CONNECTION LIFESTYLES SERIES

OVERCOMING DEPRESSION

By Skip Heitzig

Produced by

Connection Communications

ISBN 1-886324-12-3

THE CONNECTION
32222 Del Obispo
San Juan Capistrano, CA 92675
(949) 496-7411

CONTENTS

CHAPTER 1

WHERE DOES DEPRESSION COME FROM?

The word for depression originates from the Latin word depressus, "to press down." At some time everyone deals with what might be considered "normal" depression, which is defined as an involuntary reaction to loss, rejection, or disappointment. Beyond this stage of depression are more serious degrees which can result in destructive behavior and an inability to function in day-to-day life.

Some depression comes from physiological problems rooted in hormonal imbalance. Depression can also be the result of our behavior or external circumstances.

Prominent figures in the Bible were no strangers to depression: Job, Moses, Paul, and many others echoed the cry of the Psalmist in asking, "Why is my soul downcast?" Clearly, deep spiritual commitment does not bring immunity from the ravages of depression.

Depression has been known to sneak up on us as insidiously as November fog, chilling the heart and even sapping the will to get out of bed in the morning. It is often referred to as "the common cold of mental illness," costing American employers more than twenty-three billion dollars a year in absenteeism and reduced productivity. This widespread condition has been blamed on several things: the state of our world, a loss of faith in social institutions, and the deterioration of traditional family values. In short, there seems to be a dire lack of "rootedness" in our modern culture.

Christians are not immune to depression. At the top of the list of causes of depression is a spiritual enemy who wants to take the wind out of God's kids' sails and make us feel helpless. Living in a world that is hostile to the gospel doesn't make it any easier. Persecution and intolerance to the gospel message by others can make the Christian feel isolated and alone, in addition to the fact that many Christians feel guilty because they think spiritual people should never feel depressed. These folks need to read the book of Psalms or the story of Job.

From the Mountain Tops

Spiritual depression is nothing new. In fact, it is a recurrent theme throughout Scripture. Elijah was a man who, despite his great faith, fell into a time of despair and depression. Prior to this period, however, he was on top of the world, having experienced one astonishing miracle after another. When a severe drought and famine fell on the land of Israel due to the nation's flagrant idolatry, God miraculously provided for Elijah by supplying a private brook of running water and meals of bread and meat delivered to him twice daily by ravens. It was as though God brought him breakfast in bed!

During the same period, God supplied a poor widow with enough oil and flour to feed herself, her son, and Elijah for quite awhile. If that wasn't enough, when the widow's son became ill and died, Elijah carried him to an upper room and prayed, only to witness God raise the young boy back to life.

By the time Elijah made it to Mount Carmel to confront a group of antagonistic idol-worshippers, he was on a roll—his faith was at an all-time high! There on the heights, in sight of hundreds of people, Elijah called down fire from heaven that consumed the sacrifices. The people were shocked into the realization that only the one true God of Israel could pull this off. As a result, there was a sweeping revival in the nation. Elijah then ordered the prophets of Baal to be captured and executed. As an extraordinary result of this turning, God removed His judgment, and the rain commenced.

To the Valleys

After such a succession of incredible events, the last thing we would expect is to find Elijah falling into depression, but he did. In the span of four verses, we see him spiraling downward to a state of utter despair. Suicidal thoughts were even part of his dark episode:

> …And he prayed that he might die, and said, "It is enough! Now, LORD, take my

life, for I am no better than my fathers!" (1 Kings 19:4)

The extraordinary had almost become ordinary to Elijah. He started having expectations that life would always be one miracle after another, and he wasn't prepared for the dose of reality that followed. Perhaps he even thought he'd get a note from King Ahab and his wife, Jezebel, announcing that they had renounced their wickedness and turned their hearts back to God. Instead, when Jezebel learned about the execution of the false prophets on Mount Carmel, she was murderously angry:

> And Ahab told Jezebel all that Elijah had done, also how he had executed all the prophets with the sword. Then Jezebel sent a messenger to Elijah, saying, "So let the gods do to me, and more also, if I do not make your life as the life of one of them by tomorrow about this time." (1 Kings 19:1–2)

Although Elijah had experienced miraculous provision from God and had stood before the nation calling fire down from heaven, he was suddenly terrified by the threats of one woman. In one fell swoop, he went from the heights of victory to the depths of depression! I believe that Elijah's recent victories made him especially vulnerable to depression. It is one of several factors that can take us off guard.

CHAPTER 2

FACTORS LEADING TO DEPRESSION

Elijah's expectations were misplaced. He thought everyone would repent and live happily ever after. Instead, he learned there was a contract out on his life—Jezebel wanted him dead within twenty-four hours! The terrible gulf between his expectations and reality fried his spiritual circuitry, and he fled into the wilderness to be alone in his depression. He had set the outcome in mental concrete, so there was no room in his expectations for God's plan or other people's free choice.

Can you relate? Have you ever looked forward to something and had the outcome all mapped out when suddenly the plans changed? If so, you know how terribly disheartening it can be. Solomon said, "Hope deferred makes the heart sick, but when the desire comes, it is a tree of life" (Prov. 13:12). People who would like to change careers and do something more meaningful with their lives often experience this because they feel trapped by their routine and responsibilities. For others, an early, forced retirement might be the trigger for depression because they suddenly feel aimless and wonder, "What good am I?"

Some of our expectations are realistic and normal: We hope to get a good job, eventually get married and have children. Later down the road, we look forward to the leisure and travel that retirement will bring. Although these are normal expectations, there are no guarantees we will experience them. Other people may have unrealistic expectations that can bring about an even deeper depression. For instance, if I expect God to do miracles every day of my life, what happens when He doesn't? I start doubting God, and my misplaced faith can cause me to crash into depression—largely because I've set myself up for it with unrealistic expectations.

The December 1993 issue of Religion Watch reported a Vanderbilt University study which stated that Pentecostals are three times more likely than other Christians to experience major depression. Of the overall group of Christian believers, 1.7 percent experienced "serious depression" over a six-month period, whereas the rate among Pentecostals was 5.4 percent. Researchers surmise that the higher rate may be due in part to the fact that depressed people are attracted to the Pentecostal's emphasis on spiritual and physical healing. The lesson for us all is to guard against unrealistic expectations by remembering that God is sovereign; we must never presume upon His perfect will.

Focusing on the Problem

On Mount Carmel Elijah was focused on the power and greatness of his Lord. When he was in the wilderness being fed by ravens and drinking from the spring of divinely provided water, his eyes were on God and His provision. But Jezebel's murderous threat consumed his attention and overwhelmed his faith. In his panic, he viewed the enemy's power to destroy him as greater than the power of God to deliver him. Elijah must have felt like asking the question Erma Bombeck posed in the title of her best-selling book, If Life is a Bowl of Cherries, What Am I Doing in the Pits?

Elijah was in the pits because that's where his focus was—the pits! It's been well stated that our outlook is determined by our up-look. Where do you look when life unravels—at the fraying threads or at the Master Weaver?

Indulging in Self-Pity

When our selfish focus makes us the center of the universe, it's a natural progression to feel sorry for ourselves. Elijah was in the depths of self-absorption and pity when he said, "...I am no better than my fathers!" (1 Kings 19:4). There are many reasons for spiritual depression, but one of the most common is the age-old problem of selfishness!

Someone once gave this Recipe for a Miserable Life:

> "Think about yourself. Talk about yourself. Use 'I' as often as possible. Mirror yourself continually in the opinion of

others. Listen greedily to what people say about you. Expect to be appreciated. Be suspicious. Be jealous and envious. Be sensitive to slights. Never forgive a criticism. Trust nobody but yourself. Insist on consideration and respect. Demand agreement with your own views on everything. Sulk if people are not grateful to you for favors shown them. Never forget a service you may have rendered. Shirk your duties if you can. Do as little as possible for others. Love yourself supremely. Be selfish."

Elijah's focus had shifted from the Lord, to his circumstances, and then from his circumstances to himself. I've heard this condition referred to as "ingrownous eyeballitis" (ingrown eyeballs). There are times when we should examine ourselves before God and confess our sins, but we should be careful that God is the One who is always in view.

Physical Exhaustion

Another reason we succumb to depression may be so obvious that we tend to overlook it—exhaustion. By the time Elijah got down to Sinai he was weak from fatigue. The guy never stopped. On Mount Carmel he had been at a high emotional and spiritual pitch. The prophets of Baal had been killed, which was also a physical ordeal. To top it all off, he made a long journey afterwards—on foot! All in all, Elijah had exerted a tremendous amount of raw energy:

> Now it happened in the meantime that the sky became black with clouds and wind, and there was a heavy rain. So Ahab rode away and went to Jezreel. Then the hand of the LORD came upon Elijah; and he girded up his loins and ran ahead of Ahab to the entrance of Jezreel. (1 Kings 18:45–46)

That was a twenty-mile run—almost a marathon! God's hand was on him, but it was still a long trip. In chapter 19 we read that he went down to the wilderness which was seventy to one hundred and twenty miles away! He was totally wiped out.

CHAPTER 3

GOD'S ANTIDEPRESSANTS

God demonstrated His consistent love for the despairing Elijah, despite the fact that he had just experienced several failures:

> Then as he lay and slept under a broom tree, suddenly an angel touched him, and said to him, "Arise and eat." Then he looked, and there by his head was a cake baked on coals, and a jar of water. So he ate and drank, and lay down again. And the angel of the LORD came back the second time, and touched him, and said, "Arise and eat, because the journey is too great for you." So he arose, and ate and drank; and he went in the strength of that food forty days and forty nights as far as Horeb, the mountain of God. (1 Kings 19:5-8)

Elijah hadn't made a stand against Jezebel and he hadn't been in confident faith in God when he fled into the wilderness. But God didn't rebuke him. Rather, in His love, God cared for him.

Our bodies are fearfully and wonderfully made, but they are also finely balanced. When that balance is upset, problems can occur. Biochemical disturbances can contribute to depressive behavior. When there is an imbalance of the brain's neurotransmitters, or chemical messengers, problems are inevitable. Deficiencies in serotonin can disrupt sleep patterns and increase anxiety while deficiencies in norepinephrine produce fatigue or depressed moods. An increased level of the hormone cortisol can intensify reactions to fear and stress.

In short, without proper rest, our bodies become depleted and our immune system can get out of whack, setting us up for depression. Spiritual dryness can result from fatigue, chemical imbalance, or illness. Elijah's despair resulted in praying that God would kill him—a request God graciously denied. When we look back on low times of physical and mental exhaustion, we can be particularly grateful that God doesn't answer all our prayers!

God's prescription for the despondent Elijah was simple: rest. When he awoke, it was to a meal miraculously prepared for him by a sovereign, loving God! Slowly but surely, he became rejuvenated.

CHAPTER 4

GET A NEW FOCUS

In the midst of Elijah's depressive episode, God asked a question which was meant to encourage him to bare his feelings and pour out his heart to God:

> And there he went into a cave, and he spent the night in that place; and behold, the word of the LORD came to him, and He said to him, "What are you doing here, Elijah?"
> (1 Kings 19:9)

God knew exactly why Elijah was in the cave, but the question allowed Elijah to openly and honestly vent his emotions. This process also exposed Elijah's faulty thinking. He was convinced that he was the only one left in Israel who was faithful and spiritual:

> So he said, "I have been very zealous for the LORD God of hosts; for the children of Israel have forsaken Your covenant, torn down Your altars, and killed Your prophets with the sword. I alone am left; and they seek to take my life."
> (1 Kings 19:10)

God allowed him to vent his emotions, but His plan was to restore him from his attitude of self-pity to a place of being used again by God. While it is healthy to vent our feelings, by itself, it's not enough. We need to change our emotional and mental perspectives as well. Elijah was in touch with his feelings, but he was not in touch with reality. Things weren't really as bad as he thought, and he needed someone to tell him so. God's question was good medicine for Elijah because it resulted in a dose of reality.

Martin Luther's wife, Katie, understood the value of the reality check when her husband had been moping around the house for an extended period of time. His beloved wife decided she might as well dress for the occasion—in black. When Luther saw her, he asked, "Who died?" To his astonishment, she answered, "God is dead!"

"What on earth do you mean, 'God is dead?'"

"The way you've been looking lately," she quickly replied, "it must be that God has died."

Her tactic produced the needed perspective, because Martin Luther wrote on a sheet of paper the single word Vivit, which means "He Lives." When difficult times were upon him, he read that word which served as a reminder and an encouragement.

CHAPTER 5

NEW EXPECTATIONS

Once God had Elijah's attention, God set out to re-adjust Elijah's expectations. He told Elijah to go outside and stand in the presence of the Lord on the mountain:

> …And behold, the LORD passed by, and a great and strong wind tore into the mountains and broke the rocks in pieces before the LORD, but the LORD was not in the wind; and after the wind an earthquake, but the LORD was not in the earthquake; and after the earthquake a fire, but the LORD was not in the fire; and after the fire a still small voice. (1 Kings 19:11–12)

Elijah had formed unrealistic views. In contrast to what he was anticipating, God was neither in the wind nor the earthquake. Instead, the Lord re-adjusted Elijah's expectations by coming to him as "a still small voice." He was learning that God's work was sometimes an inner work of the heart.

Take Obedient Action

When Elijah was at the end of his rope, he told the Lord that he wanted to die. The Lord responded by telling him to get up and get moving: "Go, return on your way to the wilderness... and when you arrive, anoint Hazael as king over Syria" (1 Kings 19:15). God wanted him to make a choice of godly action based on obedience rather than on how he felt.

Many people believe that the pressures of life are what lead to depression. However, it's how we handle those pressures that lead us either to depression or to victory. Once we realize that we are loved unconditionally by God, our reactions to trouble and fear are brought into perspective. When depression threatens, we don't have to run to artificial means to solve the problem and raise our self-esteem. If we are obediently focused on the Lord, self-esteem is overshadowed by God-esteem, and our self-worth is anchored in Christ.